CW00393197

About The Author

Callum Rowley is a student at University College London, Studying a MSci in Natural Science. He achieved A*A*A* at A Level, including Biology, and these questions that you've been lucky enough to purchase formed a large part of his revision.
Never one to shy away from academic work, Callum continued working past his A Level exam to ensure that the material brought to you in this book was of the highest possible standard. He is also known for his work on Mental Health, publishing *'How Depression is Perceived in Young Males in the Education System and Why: A short dissertation analysing a study of 226 young males'* in January 2017.

Publishing Rights

2nd Edition

Table of Contents

Tips for using this Workbook

This workbook is filled with over 350 short answer questions, as well as the answers, which cover topics 3-8 of the AQA A-Level syllabus. It is easy to use this workbook, answer the questions, and gain very little from the experience. The following steps are how we recommend you use the workbook in order to gain as much as possible from it. Leave several days between each step.

- First, answer the questions with the help of the syllabus. This ensures you don't reinforce any mistakes. Mark this using the provided mark scheme, making sure that you write corrections to any errors out several times to hammer the points home.
- The second time you do the questions, do them without using your notes. You can spend as long as you need on them. Make sure you answer every question as best you can. Again, once done, mark and write out several times corrections for any mistake you made.
- The third time you do the questions, try and do them against the clock. Allocate yourself 15 minutes for each set of questions. Whilst this isn't long, the idea is to push yourself and force yourself to be able to answer quickly under pressure. Do corrections to fix any little errors. By this stage you should be making very few errors.
- Once you have done them three times written out, you should be at the stage where you know each question very well. Review them verbally on a weekly basis, and if you find yourself slipping, conduct step 3 again.

Organisms exchange substances with their environment - Questions

1) How does an increase in volume effect Surface Area:Volume ratio?
2) Name the process by which prokaryotes exchange gasses?
3) Name three components of the tracheal system in insects?
4) Name two components of the gas exchange system in gills of a fish?
5) By what principle do fish exchange gasses in their gills?
6) Define dicotyledonous?
7) Name two components of the leaves of dicotyledonous pants involved in gas exchange?
8) How do xerophytic plants limit water loss?
9) How do insects balance the need for gas exchange with the need to limit water loss?
10) Name three components of the lungs involved in gas exchange?
11) Over which membranes in the lungs do gasses have to pass?
12) What features do the surface over which gasses pass in the lungs have to enable efficient gas exchange?
13) Name the method of interaction between internal and external intercostal muscles?
14) Outline the movement of the diaphragm muscle in
a) Inhalation
b) Exhalation
15) What cavity is involved in gas exchange in the lungs?
16) State the equation for PVR (Pulmonary ventilation rate)?
17) What builds up in the lungs as a result of cystic fibrosis?
18) What elements of lung function are affected?
19) How do sufferers of fibrosis adjust to compensate?
20) What forms in the lungs of TB sufferers?
21) What disease does TB eventually lead to?
22) How does reducing the quantity of oxygen available affect the cells in the body?
23) What reaction occurs in which larger molecules are broken into smaller ones?
24) Why must molecules be made smaller to allow digestion?
25) What two enzymes break down carbohydrates?
26) Which enzyme breaks down lipids?
27) Explain how bile salts aid with the digestion of lipids?
28) Which three enzymes break down proteins?
29) Briefly outline how these three enzymes carry out their function?
30) Where in mammals does absorption occur?
31) What mechanism permits absorption of amino acids and monosaccharides?
32) State the equation for CO (Cardiac Output)?
33) What is the role of Haemoglobin?
34) Do all organisms have the same type of haemoglobin?
35) What is Haemoglobin made out of?
36) Which metal ion is at the centre of the haemoglobin molecule?

37)   In what cell is haemoglobin located?

38)   How does one oxygen molecule binding to haemoglobin affect the binding of other molecules?

39)   Outline the Bohr effect?

40)   How do high-altitude animals adapt to the low oxygen environment?

41)   Name the blood vessels entering and leaving (A diagram may help with this)

a)   The heart?

b)   The lungs?

c)   The kidneys?

42)   What is the function of the kidneys?

43)   How do valves aid in heart function?

44)   What connects the valves to the walls of the heart?

45)   What is an atheroma and how does it affect the artery?

46)   Describe the structure of the following, and how it relates to the function

a)   Arteries

b)   Arterioles

c)   Veins

47)   What feature of capillaries, relating to red blood cells, is important for their role as exchange surfaces?

48)   Why is fluid forced out the capillaries at the start of the capillary bed?

49)   Where is hydrostatic pressure lower, the venule end or arteriole end?

50)   How does the water potential of the blood change across the capillary bed?

51)   What system is responsible for draining the excess fluid away from the tissues and back into the circulatory system?

52)   What dead tissue in plants transports water?

53)   Outline the 4 steps of the cohesion tension theory, starting at the leaves?

54)   Which living tissue transports organic substances?

55)   Does translocation require energy?

56)   Where do solutes move from and to in translocation?

57)   How do enzymes maintain a concentration gradient in translocation?

58)   What is the name of the best supported theory for how translocation occurs?

59)   How does ringing allow scientists to investigate transport in plants?

Genetic information, variation and relationships between organisms - Questions

1) Give three ways prokaryotic DNA differs from Eukaryotic DNA?
2) What proteins are DNA molecules in eukaryotes associated with?
3) Name two organelles of Eukaryotes which contain DNA?
4) What two things do genes code for the production of?
5) Name the term for the position on a chromosome that a specific gene occupies?
6) What is meant by the term 'Degenerate code'?
7) What are the non-coding sections of DNA called?
8) Name the four different bases in DNA?
9) Which base is switched to Uracil in RNA?
10) Define:
    a) Genome
    b) Proteome
    c) Allele
11) Two sister chromatids are joined at what?
12) The section of three bases in tRNA which binds to the mRNA strand is called?
13) Give the three components of DNA?
14) What is the difference in RNA?
15) State the complementary base pairings in DNA and RNA?
16) In what process is pre-mRNA created?
17) Which enzyme in involved in this process to join RNA nucleotides together?
18) What is the DNA strand known as in this process?
19) What happens to pre-mRNA before it leaves the nuclear envelope?
20) When mRNA is in the cytoplasm, which organelle does it attach to for the next stage of protein synthesis?
21) What bond forms between two amino acids in protein synthesis?
22) What is the role of ATP in translation?
23) What is the role of tRNA in translation?
24) What is a gene mutation?
25) What difference often arises due to substitution mutations?
26) Why do some substitution mutations not affect the protein function at all?
27) In a deletion mutation, why is it unlikely that the polypeptide coded for will function correctly?
28) What is the process called in which mutations in the number of chromosomes occurs?
29) In sexual reproduction, what fuses to give rise to a new offspring?
30) What is a diploid number of chromosomes?
31) How many chromosomes do humans have?

32) Define homologous chromosomes?
33) In the first stage of meiosis, meiosis I, what separates?
34) What then separates in meiosis II?
35) Name two processes which increase genetic variation in the offspring which are a result of meiosis?
36) Outline the process which occurs in meiosis I which increases genetic variation?
37) How many haploid daughter cells are produced from one diploid parent cell?
38) Define genetic diversity?
39) Outline natural selection?
40) What causes bacteria to be resistant to antibiotics?
41) What type of selection is exemplified by antibiotic resistant bacteria?
42) Why are human birth weights an example of stabilising selection?
43) Give an example of each of these types of adaptation that can result from natural selection
    a) Anatomical
    b) Physiological
    c) Behavioural
44) Define species
45) What parts of the classification system are used to name a species?
46) Starting with Domain, list the hierarchy of classification?
47) Give two benefits to the species of courtship behaviour?
48) What is species richness a measure of?
49) What does the index of diversity look at? How is it calculated?
50) How do farming techniques effect biodiversity?
51) Give three methods that can be done to help achieve a balance between food production and conservation?
52) Name three ways in which it is possible to measure genetic diversity within or between species?
53) What is the best way to eliminate sampling bias?

Energy Transfers in and Between Organisms – Questions

1) Name two purposes of light in the light-dependent reaction?
2) By what process does chlorophyll absorb light?
3) Where are the electron carriers located?
4) Write the equation for the photolysis of water?
5) What is the enzyme embedded in the chloroplast membranes?
6) What is produced in the light dependent reaction and subsequently used in the light independent one?
7) What does CO_2 react with and what does it form in the first stage of the light independent reaction?
8) What enzyme catalyses that reaction?
9) What reduces GP to triose phosphate?
10) What two things does triose phosphate go to?
11) List three environmental factors that may limit the rate of photosynthesis?
12) What is produced by respiration?
13) What is the purpose of phosphorylating a molecule?
14) Where does glycolysis occur? Why is this the case?
15) Is glycolysis aerobic or anaerobic?
16) What is glucose phosphorylated to?
17) By what process does triose phosphate turn into pyruvate?
18) How many molecules of pyruvate are gained from one glucose molecule?
19) In anaerobic respiration, what can pyruvate be converted to?
20) By what process is pyruvate transported into the mitochondrial matrix?
21) When pyruvate is oxidised to acetate, what is produced?
22) In the link reaction, what combines with acetate?
23) What does acetylcoenzyme A react with to produce a 6 carbon molecule?
24) What is produced in the Krebs cycle?
25) Outline chemiosmotic theory?
26) What other respiratory substrates can enter the Krebs cycle?
27) What do plants use to synthesise organic compounds?
28) What is the main use of sugars produced by plants?
29) How can biomass be measured?
30) What is
   a) Gross primary production?
   b) Net primary production?
31) Give an equation linking Gross productivity, Net Productivity and respiratory losses for producers?

32) Give an equation for Net productivity in consumers involving Chemical energy stored in ingested food (I), Chemical energy lost to the environment in faeces and urine (F) and respiratory losses to the environment (R)

33) What effect does shortening a food web have?

34) Give three examples of ways to increase the efficiency of a food web in the raising of pigs on a farm?

35) Give two examples of how nutrients are recycled within ecosystems?

36) What bacteria are involved in decomposition?

37) How do these bacteria help decompose dead organisms?

38) What substances can mycorrhizae help with the uptake of?

39) What is used in ammonification to make ammonia?

40) Give the two stages of nitrification?

41) Give the two locations at which nitrogen fixing bacteria are found?

42) What conditions are required by denitrifying bacteria and when do these conditions occur?

43) What do denitrifying bacteria do?

44) What is guano?

45) Where is the main reservoir of phosphorous?

46) What natural process helps phosphate ions become dissolved and available for absorption by plants?

47) What are two advantages of natural fertilisers?

48) What are two advantages of artificial fertilisers?

49) What is leaching?

50) What is eutrophication and why is it a problem?

Stimuli and response and Nervous Coordination – Questions

1) Why do organisms respond to changes in their environment?
2) Define:
   a) Tactic response
   b) Kinetic Response
3) How do plants respond to stimuli?
4) What is IAA?
5) Where in a plant is IAA produced?
6) How does IAA effect cells in shoots and roots?
7) Outline the pathway of a simple reflex arc?
8) What three neurones are involved in a simple reflex arc?
9) What purpose does a simple reflex arc serve?
10) What do the Pacinian corpuscles detect?
11) What ion channels are present in the Pacinian corpuscles?
12) What is established when a receptor is stimulated?
13) When is an action potential triggered?
14) What is the connective tissue called that is wrapped around the sensory nerve ending in Pacinian corpuscles?
15) What two types of cells detect light in the eyes?
16) Which type of cell has high visual acuity?
17) Why do the two types of cells have different visual acuity?
18) Which of the two types of cell is most sensitive to light?
19) Which type of cell is responsible for trichromatic vision?
20) What is responsible for the blind spot of an eye?
21) What neurone connects photoreceptors to the optic nerve?
22) What is different about myogenic muscle tissue?
23) Outline the roles of the:
   a) Sinoatrial node (SAN)
   b) Atrioventricular node (AVN)
   c) Bundle of His
   d) Purkyne tissue
24) What section of the brain subconsciously controls the rate at which the SAN fires?
25) Where are the baroreceptors located and what are they stimulated by?
26) Where are the chemoreceptors located and what are they stimulated by?
27) What effectors are released to:
   a) Slow down heart rate?
   b) Speed up heart rate?

28) When low O_2, high CO_2 or low blood pH is detected, how is heart rate changed to bring back normal levels?

29) State the equation linking Cardiac Output (CO), Stroke Volume (V) and Heart Rate (R)?

30) What is a myelin sheath?

31) What cells are myelin sheaths made from?

32) What is the term for the bare patches of membrane between the cells?

33) Where are sodium ion channels concentrated at?

34) In a myelinated neurone, where does depolarisation occur?

35) How does myelination effect the speed of conduction?

36) Give two other features that would effect speed of conduction?

37) When a resting potential is established, how is the outside of a cell charged in comparison with the inside?

38) What proteins create and maintain a resting potential?

39) Why are there more sodium ions outside the cell than on the inside?

40) When a stimulus is detected, what channel proteins open?

41) What occurs when the threshold is reached?

42) When repolarisation occurs, how does the membrane permeability to sodium and potassium change?

43) What effect does the refractory period have on nervous impulses?

44) As described by the all-or-nothing principle, how would a bigger stimulus effect:
   a) The size of an action potential?
   b) The frequency at which an action potential fires?

45) What is contained in the vesicles of the presynaptic knob?

46) What is the gap between the cells at the synapse called?

47) Why are synapses unidirectional?

48) When an action potential arrives at a Cholinergic synapse, what three steps happen?

49) What is summation in relation to synapses?

50) State the names of both types of summation?

51) How is ACh removed from the synaptic junction?

52) What are stored in clefts at a neuromuscular junction?

Muscles and Homeostasis – Questions

1) State the three types of muscle in the body?
2) In an antagonistic muscle pair, which is the agonist and which is the antagonist?
3) What bundles of cells make up skeletal muscle?
4) What is the cell membrane of a muscle fibre called?
5) What does the transverse (T) tubule do?
6) What is stored in the sarcoplasmic reticulum?
7) Why do muscle fibres have lots of mitochondria?
8) Which filaments make up the dark band of a myofibril?
9) What is contained in the I bands?
10) What gets shorter when muscles contract?
11) What two binding sites are present on a myosin head?
12) What allows the myosin head to move back and forth?
13) At rest, what does tropomyosin do?
14) When an action potential from a motor neurone stimulates a muscle cell, what is depolarised?
15) What two things do Ca^{2+} ions do to allow the formation of a cross bridge?
16) By what process are Ca^{2+} ions moved back into the sarcoplasmic reticulum?
17) Give the equation for the phosphorylation of ADP by PCr?
18) What kind of exercise is the ATP-phosphocreatine system good for?
19) Is the ATP-phosphocreatine system anaerobic or aerobic?
20) Give two structural differences between slow and fast twitch muscle fibres?
21) Why is maintaining a stable homeostatic environment important?
22) What is the effect of a high temperature on enzyme activity?
23) Explain the effect on the water potential of the blood in relation to:
    a) High blood glucose concentration?
    b) Low blood glucose concentration?
24) Describe the negative feedback mechanism?
25) Why does negative feedback only function within certain limits?
26) When does blood glucose concentration rise and fall?
27) Which cells in the islets of Langerhans secrete each hormone?
28) Give the reactions for each of the following:
    a) Glycogenesis?
    b) Gluconeogenesis?
    c) Glycogenolysis?
29) Why are hormonal responses slower than nervous responses?
30) When the pancreas detects high blood glucose concentration, which hormone secretion is stopped?
31) When insulin binds to receptors on muscle cell membranes, what happens?

32) To what cells does glucagon bind?

33) Where is adrenalin secreted from?

34) When is adrenalin secreted?

35) What process is inhibited by adrenalin?

36) Outline the secondary messenger model?

37) Which two hormones are secondary messengers?

38) What enzyme is activated when these hormones bind to their receptors?

39) What is ATP then converted to?

40) What enzyme does this activate?

41) Which type of diabetes is acquired later in life and linked to obesity?

42) What cells does the immune system attack in type I diabetes?

43) How can people take steps to reduce their risk of developing diabetes?

44) How do type I diabetics control insulin levels?

45) Define osmoregulation?

46) What cells in the hypothalamus monitor the water potential of the blood?

47) When water potential of the blood is low, what hormone is released into the blood?

48) What gland releases this hormone?

49) Which cells become more permeable to water because of this hormone binding to them?

50) What are the substances that enter the Bowman's Capsule known as?

51) In selective reabsorption, where do useful substances pass from and to?

52) Where in the body is the medulla?

Genetics, populations, evolution and ecosystems – Questions

1) Define:
    a) Genotype?
    b) Phenotype?
    c) Homozygous?
    d) Codominant?
2) True or False: There is only two alleles of each gene?
3) Give three types of alleles relating to expression of characteristics?
4) What is monohybrid inheritance?
5) What is a phenotypic ratio?
6) What is epistasis?
7) Give the equation for the chi-squared value?
8) When is the chi-squared test used?
9) Define:
    a) Species
    b) Population
    c) Gene Pool
10) State the equation for genotype frequency per the Hardy-Weinberg principle?
11) Give two conditions required for the Hardy-Weinberg principle to be valid?
12) What does the Hardy-Weinberg principle predict?
13) What is the primary source of genetic variation?
14) Give three examples of environmental factors which can lead to variation?
15) What two processes can evolution occur by?
16) What is the term for pressures that affect an organism's survival chance?
17) How does the frequency of beneficial alleles change from one generation to the next?
18) Give the three types of natural selection?
19) Draw a graph illustrating each of the above
20) What is speciation?
21) How do allopatric and sympatric speciation differ?
22) Give an example of something which could cause allopatric speciation?
23) How may mechanical changes lead to reproductive isolation?
24) In what communities does evolution occur via genetic drift?
25) What is an ecosystem?
26) Give an example of as many of the following as you can:
    a) Biotic factors
    b) Abiotic Factors
27) What is a niche?

28) What happens if two species occupy the exact same niche?

29) Why may the carrying capacity of an ecosystem vary?

30) Describe the difference between interspecific and intraspecific competition?

31) How can the size of a population be estimated for:
    a) Slow-moving/non-motile organisms
    b) Motile organisms?

32) When performing the mark-release-recapture method of estimating population size, what assumptions must be made?

33) Give the equation used to estimate population size through mark-release-recapture?

34) What is meant by the phrase 'ecosystems are dynamic systems'?

35) In primary succession, what is the first species to colonise an area called?

36) How do pioneer species change the abiotic conditions?

37) When a new species moves into the area, what happens to the pioneer species?

38) What does this eventually lead to?

39) How does secondary succession differ from primary succession?

40) What is a plagioclimax?

41) Why do humans often manage succession?

42) State four ways it is possible to help conserve species?

The control of gene expression - Questions

1) Give six examples of gene mutations?
2) What effects do mutagenic agents have on the rate of mutation?
3) What can mutations result in?
4) When mutations only change one codon, why does this sometimes have no effect on the polypeptide coded for?
5) What is a frame shift?
6) What are base analogues?
7) What are:
8) Totipotent cells?
9) Pluripotent cells?
10) Multipotent/Unipotent cells?
11) What causes cell specialisation?
12) How often can pluripotent cells divide?
13) How are unipotent cells involved in the heart?
14) How are iPS cells created in the lab?
15) What is the name of the site at which activators and repressors bind?
16) How do the following effect RNA polymerase binding:
17) Activators?
18) Repressors?
19) What type of transcription factor is oestrogen?
20) Give two examples of epigenetic control of gene expression, and briefly outline each?
21) Can epigenetic changes be passed to offspring?
22) What causes epigenetic changes to DNA?
23) How does an error in epigenetic control of gene expression link to cancer?
24) Why are epigenetic causes of disease a good target for drugs?
25) What is the role of RNAi?
26) Where in cells does RNAi target the mRNA?
27) What is a tumour?
28) What do tumour suppressor genes and proto-oncogenes both do?
29) If a mutation occurs in the proto-oncogene, what happens?
30) What is a mutated proto-oncogene called?
31) What are the differences between malignant and benign tumours?
32) If the Tumour Suppressor Genes become hyper methylated, what happens, and how does this link to tumour formation?
33) Give two theories as to how increased oestrogen levels link to breast cancer?
34) How does sequencing the proteome of pathogens help with the formation of vaccines?
35) Why is it harder to determine the proteome of humans than of bacteria?

36) What feature of the genetic code, as well as transcription and translation mechanisms, means that recombinant DNA technology only requires the transfer of DNA fragments?

37) Give three methods of manufacturing DNA fragments?

38) What enzymes cut DNA strands and leave sticky ends?

39) Why is it beneficial for DNA strands to have sticky ends?

40) What is the difference between in vivo and in vitro gene cloning?

41) What is a vector?

42) Give two examples of vectors?

43) Name the enzyme used to stick the DNA fragment to the vector DNA?

44) Outline a method for identifying which cells have taken up a vector and it's DNA?

45) Why are promotor and terminator regions added to the DNA of vectors?

46) Outline the Polymerase Chain Reaction?

47) Give a benefit of transformed organisms in agriculture?

48) What is the difference between somatic and germ line gene therapy?

49) If a disease is caused by a dominant allele, how would you use recombinant DNA technology to prevent it being expressed?

50) What are DNA probes?

51) What is attached to a DNA probe?

52) List 3 uses of screening with DNA probes?

53) What is a VNTR?

54) Why do different VNTRs travel different distances in gel electrophoresis?

55) List two uses of genetic fingerprints?

Organisms exchange substances with their environment – Answers

1) Larger volume means <u>smaller SA:V ratio</u>
2) <u>Diffusion</u> due to the small diffusion pathway.
3) Spiracles, Trachea, Tracheoles
4) Gill filaments, Lamellae
5) Counter current mechanism
6) A plant in which the seed has two embryonic leaves
7) Stomata, Guard Cells, mesophyll cells
8) Waxy cuticle, Hairy leaves, curled shape, sunken stomata, reduced SA:V ratio of leaves
9) In dry conditions spiracles close to limit water loss.
10) Trachea, Bronchioles, Alveoli
11) Alveolar epithelium, Capillary epithelium
12) Thin, flattened cells so short diffusion pathway
13) Antagonistic
14)
   a) The diaphragm muscle contracts, causing it to flatten, increasing volume of thorax
   b) The diaphragm muscle relaxes, arching upwards, reducing the volume of the thorax
15) Thorax/Thoric Cavity
16) PVR = Tidal Volume x Breathing Rate
17) Mucous
18) Larger diffusion pathway
19) Increase ventilation (breathing) rate
20) Scar tissue
21) Cystic Fibrosis
22) Reduces rate of respiration.
23) Hydrolysis
24) To allow them to pass through cell membranes.
25) Amylase and membrane-bound dissacharidases
26) Lipases
27) Bile salts emulsify lipids into micelles. This increases the S.A. for lipases to act upon.
28) Endopeptidases, Exopeptidases, Depeptidises
29) Endopeptidases attack anywhere along polypeptide chain, except ends. Exopeptidases attack ends of polypeptide chain. Depeptidises break down dipeptides into single amino acids.
30) Ileum
31) Co-transport

32) CO = Heart rate x Stroke volume

33) To transport O_2 round the body

34) No.

35) 4 Polypeptide chains with an Fe ion centre

36) Fe

37) Red Blood Cell

38) It makes it easier

39) As ppCO2 increases, oxygen affinity decreases

40) They produce haemoglobin that has a higher affinity for oxygen.

41)
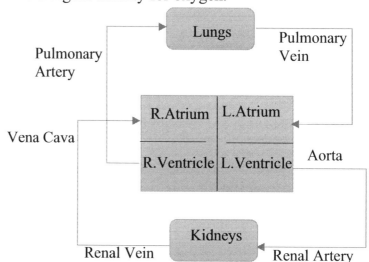
   a) See Diagram
   b) See Diagram
   c) See Diagram

42) To filter the blood

43) Prevent backflow of blood and help maintain pressure

44) Chords (Valve tendons)

45) Build up of fat/dead cells/white blood cells/connective tissue. Increases pressure as lowers size of lumen.

46)
   a) Thick muscle layer to control blood flow. Thin elastic layer to maintain high blood pressure. Overall thick wall to prevent bursting. No valves as high pressure prevents backflow.
   b) Thicker muscle than arteries. Able to control movement of blood into capillaries. Lower blood pressure than arteries so thinner elastic layer
   c) Thin muscle as not controlling blood flow to tissues. Thin elastic as low blood pressure. Thin wall as low blood pressure. Valves prevent backflow.

47) They are smaller. This pushes red blood cells right up against the capillary wall to shorten diffusion pathway.

48) Large hydrostatic pressure in capillary.

49) Venule end

50) It gets lower

51) Lymphatic system

52) Xylem

53) Water evaporates from leaves. Tension created, so water pulled into leaves from xylem. Cohesive water molecules pulled up xylem. Water enters xylem through roots.

54) Phloem

55) Yes

56) Source to Sink

57) They use up solutes at the sink, converting them to a different product to maintain a diffusion gradient.

58) Mass Flow

59) Remove a ring of bark from a stem. Accumulation of sugars above the ring causes the bank to bulge, which indicates it is the phloem in the bank which is responsible for transporting sugars.

Genetic information, variation and relationships between organisms - Answers

1) Shorter, not associated with proteins, circular
2) Histone Proteins
3) Mitochondria, Chloroplasts
4) Amino acid sequence of a peptide, functional RNA
5) locus
6) Several codons code for the same amino acid
7) Introns
8) Guanine, Cytosine, Adenine, Thymine
9) Thymine
10)
    a) The complete set of genes in a cell
    b) A full range of proteins a cell is able to produce
    c) An alternative form of a gene
11) Centromere
12) Anticodon
13) Deoxyribose 5 carbon sugar, phosphate backbone, nitrogen containing base
14) Ribose 5 carbon sugar
15) C-G, A-T. A-U in RNA.
16) Transcription
17) RNA Polymerase
18) Template strand
19) The introns are removed.
20) Ribosome
21) Peptide bond
22) Provides energy for bond to form between tRNA and the amino acid
23) Carries amino acids to the nucleotide. Lines them in correct order.
24) A change in the DNA base sequence of chromosomes
25) A single different amino acid
26) Degenerate DNA. Several codons can code for same amino acid.
27) Frame shift occurs.
28) Chromosome non-disjunction
29) Gametes
30) Number of chromosomes. A diploid is two copies of each (2n)
31) 46. 23 pairs.
32) Pairs of matching chromosomes.
33) The homologous pairs.
34) The two chromosomes in a homologous pair split up

35) Crossing over, independent segregation of chromosomes

36) Crossing over. The chromatids wrap around each other and swap bits of genetic information. This means each chromatid has the same genes but a different combination of alleles.

37) 4

38) The number of different alleles in a species/population

39) Individuals with an allele that increases survival chance are more likely to survive, reproduce and pass on their genes. This leads to an increase of allele frequency of beneficial genes, which over time leads to evolution.

40) Mutation in their DNA allows some bacteria to survive the use of antibiotics. This enables those bacteria to survive and reproduce, passing on the resistant alleles to their offspring.

41) Directional Selection

42) Babies at the extreme ends aren't able to survive.

43)
   a) Anatomical are Physical Features such as an animals shape
   b) Physiological adaptations include the ability to make venom; but also more general functions such as temperature regulation
   c) Behavioural adaptations can be inherited or learnt and include tool use, language and swarming behaviour

44) A species is a group of similar organisms that can reproduce to produce fertile offspring.

45) Genus, Species

46) Domain, Kingdom, Phylum, Class, Order, Family, Genus, Species

47) Prevents mating with members of different species. Allows members of species to know when others are ready to mate.

48) The number of different species in a community

49) The number of species and the abundance of each species in a community. $d = \dfrac{N(N-1)}{\sum n(n-1)}$

50) Reduce

51) Plant hedges between fields instead of using fences. Leaving margins around fields for wild flowers to grow. Leave fields unplanted occasionally.

52) Genome sequencing, Comparing amino acid sequences, immunological comparisons,

53) Random sampling.

Energy Transfers in and Between Organisms – Answers

1) Excites electrons in chlorophyll, leading to photoionization. Cyclic Photophosphorylation. Photolysis of water.
2) Photoionization.
3) Thylakoid membranes.
4) $2H_2O \rightarrow 4H^+ + 4e^- + O_2$
5) ATP Synthase
6) Reduced NADP, ATP
7) Reacts with RuBP to form 2xGP
8) Rubisco
9) Reduced NADP
10) Reforms RuBP, creates organic substances
11) Temperature, Light intensity, CO_2 Concentration
12) ATP
13) Make it more reactive
14) Cytoplasm. Glucose is too large to enter the mitochondria.
15) Anaerobic.
16) Glucose phosphate (Then triose phosphate)
17) Oxidation
18) 2
19) Lactate or ethanol
20) Active transport
21) Reduced NAD, CO_2
22) Coenzyme A
23) 4 carbon compound
24) 2 CO_2, 1 reduced FAD, 3 reduced NAD, 1 ATP
25) Hydrogen atoms released by reduced NAD/FAD, split up into protons and electrons. Electrons move down transport chain, transporting protons into intermembranal space of mitochondria. Protons diffuse down electrochemical gradient, driving the enzyme ATP synthase to produce ATP.
26) Proteins/Lipids
27) Energy from sunlight
28) Respiration
29) Dry mass of carbon, or dry mass of tissue per unit area per unit time.
30)
   a) Total amount of chemical energy converted from light energy by plants
   b) Gross primary productivity, with respiratory losses taken into account
31) NPP = GPP – R

32) $N = I - (F+R)$
33) Increases the efficiency
34) Restrict movement, Keep them in heated conditions, give them easier to digest food, give them antibiotics
35) Nitrogen Cycle, Phosphorous Cycle
36) Saprobionts
37) Secrete enzymes
38) Water and inorganic ions
39) Dead organisms/faecal matter
40) Ammonia/Ammonium ions to nitrites, nitrites to nitrates
41) Nitrogen fixing bacteria in root nodules, nitrogen fixing bacteria in soil
42) Anaerobic – waterlogged soil
43) Nitrates in the soil are converted to atmospheric nitrogen
44) Seagull excrement rich in phosphates
45) Rocks
46) Weathering
47) Slow release, cheaper
48) Exact composition of minerals/ions required by crops, easier to store
49) When fertiliser in the soil is washed into nearby water sources such as seas/lakes/rivers
50) When algae grows on the surface of water bodies and prevents light reaching plants below. They die and bacteria decompose them, using up the water bodies oxygen supply. This removes oxygen from the water, causing death of marine life.

Stimuli and response and Nervous Coordination – Answers

1) To increase survival chance

2)
    a) Directional response to a stimulus. Direction of stimulus effects direction of response.
    b) Movement in response to a stimulus. Intensity of stimuli effects the response.

3) Using growth factors.

4) Auxin. It is a plant hormone. It allows plants to be photo and gravotrophic.

5) The tips of roots and shoots.

6) It promotes cell elongation in shoots and restricts it in roots.

7) Stimulus – receptors – CNS – Effectors – Response]

8) Sensory neurone, replay neurone, motor neurone

9) Protective response to increase survival chance.

10) Pressure

11) Stretch-mediated sodium ion channels

12) A generator potential

13) When a generator potential exceeds a threshold

14) Lamellae

15) Rod cells and cone cells

16) Cone cells

17) Several rod cells connect to one bipolar neurone. This means they are sensitive but have low visual acuity as it isn't possible to tell which exact rod cell(s) was stimulated

18) Rod cells

19) Cone cells

20) The location where the optic nerve leaves the eye is the blind spot

21) Bipolar neurone

22) It can contract and relax without receiving signals from nerves.

23)
    a) Sends regular electrical impulses to the atrial walls to control heart rate. Causes right and left atria to contract simultaneously.
    b) Passes the impulse to the bundle of His. Has a slight delay to ensure atria are empty.
    c) This is a group of muscle fibres that conduct impulses from the ventricles to the apex.
    d) This tissue is fibres from the bundle of His. It carries waves of electrical activity into the ventricle walls, causing simultaneous contraction from the bottom up.

24) Medulla

25) Aorta and Carotid arteries – Pressure.

26) Aorta, carotid arties and medulla. O_2 levels, CO_2 levels and Ph (which indicates O_2 level)

27)
    a) Acetylcholine, which binds to receptors on the SAN.

b) Noradrenaline, which binds to receptors on the SAN.

28) Heart rate is increased. This is done by releasing noradrenaline.

29) CO = V x R

30) An electrical insulator

31) Schwann cells

32) Nodes of Ranvier

33) Nodes of Ranvier

34) Nodes of Ranvier

35) Increases it all less depolarisation has to occur.

36) Temperature, Axon Diameter

37) It is positively charged.

38) Potassium ion channels, Sodium/Potassium pumps

39) They are actively transported out, and the cell membrane is not very permeable to them.

40) Na^+ channels

41) Lots more Na^+ channels open

42) Impermeable to sodium, permeable to potassium.

43) Acts as a time delay so impulses don't overlap. Ensures impulses are discrete. Means there's a limit to how often impulses can fire.

44)
   a) No change
   b) Faster frequency

45) Neurotransmitters

46) Synaptic cleft

47) Only the post-synaptic neurone has receptors

48) Ca^{2+} ions move into presynaptic knob. Vesicles with ACh fuse with membrane of synapse, releasing neurotransmitter. This diffuses across the synaptic cleft and activates the receptors. The neurotransmitter is then broken down by AChE

49) Where the effect of many neurones, or one stimulated multiple times, is added together.

50) Spatial summation, Temporal summation

51) AChE breaks it down, and the products are reabsorbed by the presynaptic neurone

52) AChE

Muscles and Homeostasis – Answers

1) Smooth, Cardiac, Skeletal
2) Agonist – contracting. Antagonist – relaxing.
3) Muscle fibres
4) Sarcolemma
5) Help spread electrical impulses through the sarcoplasm
6) Calcium ions
7) To provide ATP for muscle contraction
8) Thick myosin filaments and some overlapping actin filaments
9) Actin filaments
10) Sarcomere
11) Actin binding site, ATP binding site
12) Hinge
13) Blocks actin from binding to the myosin-actin binding site
14) Sarcolemma. This spreads down T tubules to the sarcoplasmic reticulum.
15) Bind to tropomyosin, changing its shape and thus preventing it from blocking the binding site. They also activate ATP Hydrolase, releasing energy to cause the myosin head to bend, allowing muscle contraction.
16) Active transport
17) ADP + PCr -> ATP + Cr
18) Short intense bursts, such as a tennis serve.
19) Anaerobic
20) Slow twitch fibres have lots more mitochondria to supply energy over a long period. They have plentiful blood supply to allow respiration.
21) To ensure enzymes have the optimal environment in which to function.
22) Speed it up, until the point where H-bonds break and the enzyme denatures
23)
   a) High blood glucose concentration means a low water potential of the blood, so water diffuses out of the cells and into the blood via osmosis. This can cause cells to die.
   b) If blood glucose concentration is low, water potential is high. There won't be enough glucose for cells to respire effectively.
24) The level of a substance is too high or low, receptors detect the change and communicate with the cells via either the nervous or hormonal system to have the effectors respond the bring the change back to normal levels.
25) If a change is too big, the effectors cannot counteract the change
26) Rises after eating, falls when exercising
27) Alpha cells secrete glucagon, beta cells secrete insulin
28).
   a) Glucose -> Glycogen – activated by insulin

b) Glycerol/Amino Acids -> Glucose – Activated by glucagon

c) Glycogen -> Glucose – Activated by glucagon

29) Hormones must travel through the blood.

30) Glucagon secretion is stopped

31) They become more permeable to glucose, as vesicles with GLUT4 proteins fuse with the cell membrane

32) Receptors

33) Adrenal glands

34) Low concentration of glucose in blood, when stressed, when exercising

35) Glycogenesis

36) A hormone binds to receptors on the outside of cells. This activates an enzyme inside of the cell, which then produces a chemical known as a secondary messenger. This allows non-lipid soluble hormones to effect the inside of cells.

37) Adrenalin, Glucagon

38) Adenylate cyclase

39) Cyclic AMP (cAMP)

40) Protein kinase A which breaks down glycogen to glucose

41) Type 2

42) Beta cells in the islets of Langerhans

43) Exercise, eat less sugar

44) Insulin pens, Controlling diet

45) Regulating the water levels of the blood

46) Osmoreceptors

47) ADH (antidiuretic hormone)

48) Posterior pituitary gland

49) Cells in the walls of the DCT and collecting duct

50) Glomerular filtrate

51) They leave the tubules of nephrons and enter the capillary network wrapped around them.

52) The kidneys

Genetics, populations, evolution and ecosystems – Answers

1)
- a) The different alleles an organism has
- b) The characteristics an organism has as a result of it's genotype
- c) When two copies of the same allele are present at a locus
- d) When both alleles are expressed in the phenotype as neither are recessive

2) False – Each person only usually has two alleles, but many can exist

3) Dominant, recessive, codominant

4) Inheritance of a characteristic controlled by a single gene

5) The ratio of different phenotypes in the offspring

6) When an allele of one gene blocks the expression of another

7) $x^2 = \sum \dfrac{(O-E)^2}{E}$ Where O=Observed result, E= Expected result

8) To see if the results of an experiment support a theory

9)
- a) A group of similar organisms that can reproduce to give fertile offspring
- b) A group of organisms of the same species living in a particular area at a particular time. They must have the potential to interbreed.
- c) The complete range of alleles in a population.

10) p2 +2pq + q2 = 1

11) A large population with no immigration, emigration, mutations or natural selection. There must be random mating – all possible genotypes can breed with all others.

12) The frequency of alleles in a population won't change from one generation to the next.

13) Mutation

14) Food, Climate, Lifestyle

15) Genetic Drift and Natural Selection

16) Selection pressures

17) It increases

18) Stabilising selection, Directional selection, disruptive selection

19) .

20) The development of a new species from an existing species

21) Allopatric requires populations to be geographically isolated, sympatric is in populations that aren't isolated from one another

22) Formation of a river on a landscape

23) Change in shape of reproductive organs means two groups of a species can no longer engage in reproduction.

24) Small ones

25) All the organisms living in a community, plus all the abiotic conditions in the area in which they live
26)
   a) Predator presence, abundance of food
   b) Temperature, Water abundance, O_2 abundance, CO_2 abundance, Nutrient availability
27) A niche is the role a species plays in its environment
28) They compete till one dies out or till one adapts to occupy a different niche
29) Abiotic and biotic factors may change, making it more/less hostile.
30) Interspecific is when organisms of different species compete for the same resource. Intraspecific is when organisms of the same species do so.
31)
   a) Using quadrats or transects placed at random intervals
   b) Using nets or other methods to capture organisms, marking, releasing and recapturing.
32) The sample has enough time to reintegrate with the population. The marking hasn't affected the individual's survival chance. There are no changes to population size due to births, deaths or migration during the study.

33)

Number caught in 1st sample   X   Number caught in 2nd sample
Number marked in 2nd sample

34) They are constantly changing
35) Pioneer Species
36) They make them less harsh
37) It is outcompeted
38) A Climax Community
39) It starts on land that has had organisms on previously
40) When succession is stopped artificially by humans
41) To conserve species
42) Managing succession, Seed banks, Captive breeding, Fishing Quotas, Protected Areas

The control of gene expression – Answers

1) Substitution, Deletion, Addition, Duplication, Inversion, Translocation
2) Increase
3) A change in the sequence of amino acids
4) DNA code is degenerate
5) When a mutation causes all the amino acids after the site of mutation to change
6) A chemical that can substitute for a base in DNA.
7)
    a) Cells that can mature into any type of body cell
    b) Cells that can mature into any type of body cell, except placental cells
    c) Cells that can divide into a limited number of cell types
8) Only part of the DNA is transcribed and translated.
9) Unlimited number of times
10) The heart has a supply which are used for repair
11) Scientists take specialised adult cells and 'reprogram' them to express transcription factors normally associated with pluripotent stem cells.
12) Promotor sites
13)
    a) They make it easier
    b) They make it more difficult/stop it happening
14) Activator
15) Increased Methylation – Methyl group attaches to CpG site. This changes DNA structure so the gene is not expressed. Decreased Acylation – When histone proteins are acylated, it is easier for the DNA to be transcribed and the genes to be expressed. Less acylation means the DNA is more tightly bound, and thus it is harder for the DNA to be transcribed.
16) Yes
17) Environmental factors and disease
18) Abnormal methylation of tumour suppressor genes/protooncogenes prevents them from functioning as they should, and allows uncontrolled cell division
19) They are reversible
20) RNAi prevents mRNA strands from being translated into proteins. It does this by physically blocking translation, before moving the mRNA to a processing body to be degraded or stored.
21) Cytoplasm
22) A mass of abnormal cells
23) Tumour suppressor genes produce a tumour suppressor protein that prevents cell division or causes apoptosis. Protooncogenes produces a protein that enables cells to divide at a controlled rate.
24) The gene becomes over active and produces lots of proteins that cause uncontrolled cell division.

25) A mutated protooncogene is called an Oncogene.
26) Malignant tumours are cancerous, grow rapidly and invade surrounding tissue. Cells can break off and spread through the body.
27) The genes that code for tumour suppressor protein are not transcribed. This means cell division increases.
28) It stimulates breast cells to divide. More divisions mean more chance of cancerous cells forming. Oestrogen may be able to induce mutations directly in cells.
29) It allows identification of the antigens on the pathogens surface.
30) Humans have introns and regulatory genes.
31) They are universal.
32) Using reverse transcriptase, using restriction endonuclease enzymes, using a gene machine
33) Restriction endonuclease
34) To enable them to be inserted into a complementary section of a vector
35) In vivo cloning is done by making the recombinant DNA, transforming the host cell and then identifying the host cells which have taken up the DNA. In Vitro uses the Polymerase Chain Reaction to make millions of copies in just a few hours.
36) Something used to transfer DNA into a cell
37) Plasmids, bacteriophages
38) DNA ligase
39) Insert a marker gene for GFP into the vector DNA. And transformed bacteria will possess the green florescent protein and subsequently will glow florescent green.
40) To allow the transformed host cells to produce proteins coded for by the DNA fragment.
41) A mixture is set up containing DNA sample, free nucleotides, primers and DNA Polymerase. It is heated to 95°C to break the hydrogen bonds between the DNA strands, then cooled to 50-60°C so primers can bind. The mix is heated to 72°C so DNA polymerase can line up free nucleotides alongside the template and form new complementary strands.
42) Increased crop yield, crops produce more vitamins/nutrients
43) Germ line is done on sex cells, somatic is done on adult cells
44) Insert 'junk' DNA into the dominant allele to prevent it from functioning.
45) Short strands of DNA used to identify is someone has an allele of a gene
46) A label
47) Identify inherited conditions, determine how a patient will respond to drugs, identify health risks
48) A non-coding base sequence that repeats over and over.
49) Longer ones are heavier and so travel less distance
50) Determining who the father of a child is, identifying if a person committed a crime.

Printed in Great Britain
by Amazon